logica et philosophia interrogans

By Lamonte Wilson Mills, Phd, ThD, LCPT, NCPT4

CONTENTS

PREFACE

PREFACE

This books purpose is to approach thoughts which exist and consider similar thoughts that would formulate in an objective form. This notwithstanding the basic understandings of the language of logic. This is not meant as a textbook, yet would be welcomed as such. For learning is merely a perspective of collected attributes limited by the silence offered at the end of questions. If there be any limit therefore, let this be the limit to this work, that the sum of understanding should begin with questions. I chose to say begin, because learning should be the possibility to shape questions with answers. Philosophers may disagree on many things. However, they may not disagree on the need for philosophy. The intent of this work is to make statements which cause for examination of the current status of philosophy (not necessarily among the scholars, but instead of those who need it.) The offering here is nothing less than something more. Therefore, read with confidence, the warranty is available, but accessible only to those who can see through the scope of logic. For time has a father with the best interest of his creation and children in mind. This is logic in the form of its best attempt by the commonality of man with his greatest of ideas.

LWM

I

1.1

Logic attempts to understand the sequences of thought in the world

1.2

The world cannot be explained by logic alone

1.3

Logic is the determined once the world has been acknowledged

1.4

To acknowledge the world, one must first determine that the world can be understood

1.5

When the world is understood Logic becomes the space which facts can be harvested, grow and produce

its life form.

1.6

Factuality is the powerhouse of logic

1.7

Facts exist, lies are an attempt at such a cause

1.8

The fact that logic exist cannot be proven because the world exist. Instead the World exist that the

proven facts may logically determine that the existence of the World is a cause for consideration of a life

formed in the space where logic began to exist.

II

2.01

Philosophy is a time stamped in space

2.02

Philosophical is not attributed to us through nature nor its greatest of vice

2.03

In philosophy nothing is possible, except the impossible. For in the mind and through the heart we discover what remains closest to our pride. Yet in the heart and through the mind we discover the author of it.

2.04

Addressing the issues forms the picture of a roughly spoken word. The words which are spoken are that of a picture mishandled and a mouth which remains silent. Still (picture), the issue(s) remain. They (the issues) are the property of silence of a picture that cannot speak.

2.05

If philosophical men wore there trousers with bow ties, the common occurrence would be yet uncommon. However, it still would have occurred, the color of any philosophy is never clear. Until it becomes simple and simplicity uses a bushel of colors.

2.001

Either a man is committed to his thoughts and thought to be sane or he is left to his sanity and those who exist with him may very well in a time to come question his sanity.

2.002

When philosophy combines the impossiblilty of insanity with the possibility of facts, we may share in the sum of reality. This reality is a picture which its frame determines the space unto which our reasoning may hold. A committed man to his reason, seems reasonable until the reasonable man uncommitted to his reasonability convinces us otherwise.

2.003

If philosophy was to divide the lines of reason and logic, philosophy would determine if the picture that is seen is a defining reality in an unstable application.

2.004

Within the division of reasoning philosophy and logic establishes its form as the facts dictate. Facts are discovered and in discovering they can be considered learned.

2.005

The object of perfection is said to be subjected to the truth. Yet those whom hold the truth subjects us all to a perfection. The perfection that we are subjected to cannot be merely learned. This perfection is not ONLY found in philosophy, nor is is ONLY found in logic, nor facts alone. Instead perfection should not be an object. Perfection is being with the absence of objection

III

30.1

What is it to think?

30.2

Is thinking something conducted with and without a purpose

30.3

Does the purpose of thinking represent a thing more than purpose?

30.4

How are thoughts constructed? Are thoughts constructed in a form of a particular style?

30.5

Thinking requires a skill. Though the unskilled may attempt such a task. Could the world be undisciplined in this attempt at this skill? How could we know if this to be true? The style of thought verse the skilled thinker with style.

30.6

The introduction of the thinker to the styled risk taker still should be with a purpose. The purpose should be determined by the skilled thinker, with consideration that risk taker has a purpose also. The risk taker determines the need for the purpose, the skilled thinker is to confirm the need.

IV

401.1

The complexity of objectivity is propositional and purposeful in that subjectivity remains either a close ally or a closer enemy.

402.3

An objective view is perhaps a view with its purpose in the identification of an object. This object becomes the subject of purpose, not only in its existence, but in its understanding of existence.

403.2

The complexity of subjectivity is purposeful in its proposition.

402.2

For subjectivity the purpose is the complexity. The subject depends on the author of its suggestion. The author though can only present the subject, thus subjecting himself to the purpose of something much greater then the subject itself.

404.5

What then is the purpose of objectivity other than merely the subject? It would seem subjective that the object of one's subjectivity purpose should not only, but certainly could be found in the object of purpose.

V

5

Logic is an elementary form of understanding utilizing the format of consisitency

5.1

To be consistent, logic requires accountability in forms of thought notwithstanding conclusions.
Formatted thinking is a friendship to the scale of thinking offered to the index of descriptive symbols.

5.2

Symbolic descriptions index some, not all thoughts. The forms of thinking which lead to conclusions
are scaled first and offered as an antedote to those who's attention forms around the visual objectivity of
a result dependent ONLY upon the scale of conclusions.

5.3

Constructing a thought at length or at short still requires some attention to the details of logic. Logic
should accompany any course of thinking seeking a correspondence of a particular conclusion. Despite
the conclusion, the course of its (logic) journey remains relevant with the partakers of the formation.

5.4

Logic is not merely a way of thinking. It is a conclusion of gathered thoughts used as application of a
future cluster of ideas.

5.5

The function of concepts is gathered at the inquiry

5.6

The concept of function as an inquiry gathered with ideas.

With authority the application of these ideas become something more. when the idea itself maintains the

logical conclusion when the construction of thought becomes only a theory.

6.008

What is the picture?

6.0008

The picture of what something is, is revealed first where?

6.08

Is what is in a picture the location of what is revealed?

6.8

Is reality modeled when a picture is defined?

6.80

Reality is but a picture of something... what is this something if we are forced to live in some form of

reality?

6.800

Does reality represent a picture of something? This something that is pictured, does the something

define reality?

6.808

The length of time one spends in understanding reality could be described as what form?

7.844

Unto the measure of such things, with a quarrel in the form of verbage how does any form of argumentation suspend the curiosity to know? The details of logic must not remain independent of the form holiness. Holiness is perhaps the measure pertaining to logic that cannot be assessed as a logical development. Instead, it is measured by something greater then thinking. It is at length the delivery of a presence which exist through the form though, physical and spiritual form. Must it remain something more, to bring gratitude and justification for those or that which requires something less?

7.3344

Into the storm the gates of days, the place of ways, the measure of pathways. A poem is never treated poorly, it can be read poorly by a fellow with a drink and no bottle to hold such. An argument can be formed with a perspective quite unfamiliar with the irony of reality.

7.460

The final thought to have and begin with having a thought.

7.899

With the personal history of the public future, we must know that evil will remain that which has chosen to live backwards.

7.900

Concluding the dream is no longer the reality. The reality was the dream. For the pursuit of the dream is logical for those who know. Those who know can dream, those who just learn may only know.

8.0

In the Beginning... God. Questions if any remains the need. The need for questions for many remains the thing. An answer to those who thirst, a drink for those who hunger. Fill your soul and empty your belly. The Son of Man lingers but more than a coat of arms, armed with a Robe of eternity. A white horse, a white house, built to stand beyond the white clouds. He has come that He may Rise. We stand in the world of compromise decisions, theories, face to face with facts. Chose wisely, but still chose.

The chose was never ours, the reason was always available.

8.10

As we spend time, we do recognize that time spent is a wage paid for by whom?

8.200

The great escape is never an exit. The great escape is the entrance. When one escapes, one is entering into a version of time that reminds us that both the exit and entrance can potentially equal something considered to be great.

8.3000

Dragons do not exist. Thus says the math professor. Dragons do exist says the art professor. In your profession a pencil and a brush both may exist, but the curiosity that guides that pencil or brush is equally limited to the problem. For the math professor, the amount of dragons that do not exist would serve his conversation with the art professor well. For the art professor the color of the dragon may very well serve the math professor well.

9.25

In logic the thing itself may only be itself, if truth is the premise. In philosophy the thing may be something other than its self if the rationale by being something other than itself is possible that it can be explained.

9.50

Why does the dictionary get so little credit?

9.75

Order and just are two sympathizing methods which constitute order. The dictionary is written in an orderly and just way however, it cannot be read as a book. Though as of this day it is still considered a book. I suspect this is because it is orderly and just. Give credit where credit is due. However, if there could be considered a problem. Perhaps it is that each and every word used to describe the dictionary... can be found in its pages. This seems orderly and just. Just not in order.

10

The picture of the sky cannot be taken. This is of course, unless the sky could cover the landscape of the lens.

11

Something beautiful can be said and also seen. Which of the two could provide the greater description?

12

The usage of an iron the iron a shirt that reads *Irony at use* is (of course a mathematician would be the expert here since we introduced the word) equal to a fruit basket with sliced tomatoes.

12.08

When the bell rings the sound that is heard is not that of a bell, it is the sound that the bell produces. Much like logic, the bell represents answer. The sound is more importantly the question to the answer of the bell.

12.10

If money is exchanged for goods, would the goods become or remain a "good" thing? Equally, if all is "good" why may we at times speak so horribly of a "good" thing.

Notes of Consideration

These notes are thoughts and considerations on a variety of issues and topics which support the application of Philosophy across and parallel with the requirement of thinking.

How does one begin to understand to teach? To teach is not just a noble attempt of justification among our fellow mankind. To teach is to fulfill the absence of thought among a world of universal curiosity. This curiosity may be fulfilled through social distinctions, philosophical complexities, imaginative mystery & intrigue, and perhaps even through the absolute nature of mathematical antidotes. Despite the frame of reference, one may safely conclude, that to adequately measure any requirement to teach this effort should be built upon the teach(er) s willingness to understand.

To teach anything, one must understand. To understand, the truth needs to be available. It is never enough to learn what something isn't. We must sacrifice our pride to draw as close and intellectually possible to understand and learn what something is. Though epistemologically, we may find our methodology of knowing, only after we determine what something is. Therefore, I shall begin with logic and truth.

LOGIC & TRUTH

We all have a philosophy. This philosophy we own constitutes and governs much of our thinking. Should we find ourselves in a position to come to certain conclusions we evoke our philosophical perspectives through and with the rules of logic and reasoning. Steven B. Cowan & James S. Speigel put it this way:

Logic is the primary tool of philosophers. In logic, the philosopher has a set of basic rules and principals for governing his thinking, for dictating when and how to draw conclusions from other things believed, and for evaluating the views of others. Logic, in other words, constitutes a science of reasoning.[1]

In learning we should know that there is a measure. This measure has a formula and that formula keeps those whom understand with a way to assess, new material. I have found one of the most significant dangers in the modern views of Christianity is the New Age movement. While its efforts have become wildly popular in the form of services on Sunday mornings, it also have begun to shape the educational process. How does the parent, teacher, student protect themselves from such an onslaught of demonic material?

---

[1] Steven B. Cowan and James S. Spiegel, *The Love of Wisdom: a Christian Introduction to Philosophy / Steven B. Cowan, James S. Spiegel.* (Nashville, TN: B&H Academic, 2009), 17.

Furthermore we face a structured demise of philosophical and logical framework which have helped to shape our laws that govern mankind with the postmodern movement. This postmodern movement has attempted to discredit the very foundation of the absolute perspectives which govern thoughts, feelings and emotions. Dr. John Warwick Montgomery suggests:

> Postmodernism, admittedly, is an amorphous phenomenon—rather like the New Age mentality: exceedingly difficult to pin down owing to the fact that its adherents and fellow travelers do not maintain a single credo. But one of the most helpful analyses of the phenomenon has been provided by D. E. Polkinghorne, who identifies four basic themes: (1) foundationlessness, (2) fragmentariness, (3) constructivism, and (4) neo-pragmatism. The Postmodernist, in maintaining that no concrete epistemic foundation exists, focuses on the immediate and the local, not on any general truths (since there are none); for him or her, the only reality is the product of one's personal constructs and the question is never whether x is true but whether by accepting x one will arrive at a satisfactory outcome.[2]

The task to think is one that would be found favorable under simplicity. Yet thinking is nothing but simple. It is an automated action in result to the collected activity associated with the inward display of an outward action. Logic is the myth and knowledge is the legend. Perhaps, the teacher would be well served to forgo the legendary status to imagine what could be in the mythological world which legends call home.

---

[2]http://www.jwm.christendom.co.uk/Files/JWM%20A%20Short%20and%20Easie%20Method%20with%20Postmodernists.pdf

LATIN VERSION

logica et philosophia interrogans

Hoc libris propositum est accedere ad cogitationes quae sunt, et intelligas, similes cogitationes, quod esset conficiet obiective in forma. Hoc tamen basic intellectus de lingua logica. Hoc non intelligitur, ut artem, tamen esset excepit, ut talis. Nam doctrina est tantum respectu collecta attributa limitata per silentium obtulit in fine quaestiones. Ut si quis medicus ergo hoc sit finis, ut hoc opus, quod summa prudentia debet incipere cum quaestiones. Elegi dicere incipiunt, quia doctrina esse posse, ut figura quaestiones cum responsionibus. Philosophi, ut dissentiant in multa. Autem, ut non dissentiunt opus philosophia. Animo hoc opus est, ut ista, quae causam pro quaestione de current status de philosophia (non necessario inter scolares, sed pro his, qui indigent.) Oblatio hic est, nihil minus quam aliquid magis. Igitur legere cum fiducia, suspendisse sit amet, sed pervia tantum ad eos, qui potest videre per ambitum logica. Nam tempus habet a patre, cum expediat suae creationis, et filios, et in mente. Hoc est logicae in forma eius optimus conatus per communitas hominis cum ejus maximum of ideas.

LWM

Ego

1.1

Logica conatus intelligere sequentia ex cogitatione in mundo

1.2

Mundus non potest explicari logica solus

1.3

Logica est determinatum semel mundo fuerit agnoscitur

1.4

Ad agnoscendam mundi, oportet prius determinare, quod in mundo potest intelligi

1.5

Cum mundus intelligitur, est Logica fit in spatio, quae res metuntur, crescere, et ipsius vitae forma.

1.6

Factuality est powerhouse logica

1.7

Facta sunt, mendacia sunt conatum in tali causa

1.8

Quod logica esse non potest probari, quia in mundo sunt. Sed in Mundo esse, quod probatur factis, ut logice determinare, quod esse in Mundo, est causa, quia consideratio de vita formatur in spatium, ubi logica coepit esse.

II

2.01

Philosophia est a tempore coagulatus in spatium

2.02

Philosophica non tribuitur nobis per naturam, neque eius maxima vice

2.03

In philosophia, nihil est possibile, nisi impossibile. Enim in mente, et per cor et nos invenire quod manet proxime ad nostra superbia. Tamen in cor, et per mentis invenimus auctor.

2.04

Alloquitur exitibus formas pictura a dure locutus est verbum. Verba, quae locutus es quod a picture mishandled et os quae restat silentium. Adhuc (picture), exitus(s) manent. (Exitus) proprium de silentio a pictura, ut loqui non possit.

\

2.05

Si philosophica viros vestitos ibi braccis, cum arcus cognationibus, communis rei esset, tamen raro. Autem, adhuc esset facta, color ullus philosophia est, non patet. Donec efficitur simplex et simplicitate utitur modio de coloribus.

2.001

Aut homo est commissa cogitationes eius et cogitatione esse sanus aut ipse est, sinistram ipsius, et sanitas, et qui sunt cum eo, ut bene in tempore venire quaestio eius sanitatem.

2.002

Cum philosophia componit impossiblilty de insania, cum possibilitatem rerum, ut nos participes in summa veritate. Hoc constitutum est a pictura, quae in eius corpore determinat spatium, ad quod nostra ratio, ut tenere. Commiserunt homo, ut eius causa, videtur rationabile donec rationabile homo verum deierat eius reasonability persuadet nobis aliter.

2.003

Si philosophia est dividere rectae rationis et logica, philosophia, esset determinare si in pictura est visa est a definitione re instabiles velit.

2.004

In divisione ratio philosophia et logica statuatur eius forma, sicut res dictare. Facta sunt inventa, et in cognitione non potest esse didicit.

2.005

Ad tertium dicendum quod perfectio dicitur esse virtuti veritatis. Tamen, quos tenere veritatem subditos nos omnes ad perfectionem. Perfectionem, quod nos sunt subiecta non solum didicit. Hoc perfectionis est non SOLUM invenitur in philosophia, nec SOLUM invenitur in logica, nec rerum solum. Sed perfectio non debet esse obiectum. Perfectio est quod, cum sine contradictione

III

30.1

Quid est cogitare?

30.2

Est cogitans aliquid deduxit cum et sine causa

30.3

Facit ad propositum ratus repraesentat rem magis quam voluntas?

30.4

Quam sunt cogitationes construitur? Sunt cogitationes constructa in a forma, ut a specie genus?

30.5

Ratus requirit arte. Si unskilled, ut conatum tale munus. Potuit mundum esse undisciplined in hoc

conatu in hac arte? Quomodo possumus scire si hoc verum? Stilo cogitatio versu peritus excogitatoris

cum style.

30.6

Introductio in excogitatoris ad appellatos periculo accipientis tamen debet esse propositum. Causa debet esse determinatum, per peritus excogitatoris, cum eo, quod periculo accipientis habet propositum etiam. Periculo accipientis determinat opus est ad propositum, peritus excogitatoris est confirmare opus.

IV

401.1

Intricata obiectivum est propositional et industria in subiectiva manet, aut prope socium vel a propinquus hostis.

402.3

An objective visum est fortasse visum est, cum eius rei causa in idem obiectum. Hoc obiectum fit subiectum propositum, non tantum in sua existentia, sed in eius intellectus esse.

403.2

Intricata subiectiva est industria in sua propositione.

402.2

Nam subiectiva propositum est complexionem. Subiectum dependet auctor eius sententia. Auctor tamen non possunt, nisi adest subiecto, sic subiiciat se ad propositum, quod multo maius, deinde in re ipsa.

404.5

Quid ergo est in causa obiectivum alterum, quam solum subiectum? Videtur subiectiva, quod obiectum

unius est subiectiva propositum, ut non solum, sed certe inveniri potuit in obiectum propositum.

V

Quinque

Logica est an elementary forma intellectus adhibendis format consisitency

5.1

Ad esse stat, logica eget nibh in formas cogitatione tamen conclusiones. Formatted ratus est amicitia, ut scala ratus offertur index descriptionum symbola.

5.2

Typicus nibh index quidam, non omnes cogitationes. Formae cogitandi quae ducunt ad conclusiones sunt conscendere primum obtulit, ut antedote iis, qui operam formas circa condimentum obiectivum de quo fit dependens SOLUM super scala conclusiones.

5.3

Struere cogitatione tandem vel ad breve tamen quodam operam ad details de logica. Logica debet comitari quis cursus ratus, quaerens a correspondentia aliqua conclusio. Quamvis conclusio, scilicet eius (logica) iter manet pertineret, cum communicantes de formatione.

5.4

Ratio est, non tantum a modo cogitandi. Est conclusio congregati cogitationes amet application futura

est botrus ideas.

5.5

Munus conceptus est congregata in inquisitione

5.6

Conceptus munus, ut inquisitio congregati cum ideas.

Cum auctoritate usus, et de his quae fieri aliquid magis. cum idea se tenet conclusio cum constructione

cogitatio fit solum a theoria.

6.008

Quid est figura?

6.0008

Picture of quod aliquid est, est revelatum primum ubi?

6.08

Est, quod est in picture situm quod est revelatum est?

6.8

Est rerum exemplar, cum a picture definitur?

6.80

Veritas est, sed imaginem aliquid... quid est hoc aliquid, si cogimur vivere in aliqua re?

6.800

Non rem repraesentant imaginem aliquid? Hoc aliquid, id est picta, facit aliquid definire

rem?

6.808

Longitudo temporis unus, expendit in intellectu, re, posset dici quod forma?

7.844

Ad mensuram huiusmodi, cum contentio in forma verbage quomodo aliqua forma argumentation suspendere curiositate scire? Details of logica non debet manere sine forma sanctitatis. Sanctitas est fortasse mensuram pertinent ad logicam, quod non potest aestimari quod rationis eget. Instead, mensuratur per aliquid maius ergo ratus. Est tandem partus praesentiae, quae esse per formam, quamvis, corporalis et spiritualis formam. Oportet eam manere plus aliquid, ferre gratiam et iustificationem, quia qui aut id quod requirit aliquid minus?

7.3344

In tempestas portas dies, loco et modo, mensura meatus. Carmen est, nunquam male agitur, potest esse legitur, male a civibus cum a bibendum et nulla ampulla tenere talis. Argumentum potest formari cum prospectu admodum consetetur sadipscing elitr, cum ironia re.

7.460

Ultima cogitavi ut et initium habens a cogitatione.

7.899

Cum alio historia publica futurum, oportet scire quod malum manebit quod elegit vivere retrorsum.

7.900

Decernentes somnium est, non veritas. Res esset somnium. Pro studio somnium est rationis et pro illis,

qui sciunt. Qui scire potest somnium, qui modo scire potest nisi sciat.

8.0

In Principio... Deus. Quaestiones si quis remanet opus. Opus quaestionum multis manet res. Responsum ad eos, qui sitit, potum pro iis, qui fame. Imple anima tua, et vacuum ventrem. Filius Hominis moratur, sed plus quam tunicam arma, armati, cum Uestimento aeternitatis. Albus equus, alba domo, aedificavit stare ultra candida nubes. Ipse venit, ut Ipse, ut Surgere. Nos stare in mundo compromissum decisiones, sententias, facie ad faciem cum rerum. Elegit sapienter, sed tamen elegit. Quod elegit, non nostra, causa erat semper sit amet.

8.10

Sicut et nos vacare, nos agnoscere, ut tempus est merces solvit per quem?

8.200

Magni fuga numquam est exitum. Magna effugium est ostium. Cum unus effugit, unum est intrare in a version of tempus admonet, quod et exitum et introitum potest potentia aequalis aliquid esse magna.

8.3000

Dracones non sunt. Hæc dicit math professor. Dracones sint, inquit, arte professor. In tua professione plumbum et dignissim utrumque potest esse, sed curiositate, ut duces, qui penicillo vel dignissim est aeque, cursus consequat. Math professor, quantum dracones, qui non sunt, servirent eius colloquium cum arte professor bene. Enim artis professor color draco, ut bene servire math professor bene.

9.25

In logica ad rem ipsam, ut tantum se, si verum est praemissa. In philosophia res sit aliud quam eius se, si rationem, per hoc quod aliquid aliud quam ipsa est possibile, quod potest exponi.

9.50

Quare dictionary, ut sic parum credit?

9.75

Ut et iustus duo sunt sympathizing rationes, quae efficiunt ordinem. Ipsum scriptum est in ordinate et iustum modo tamen, non erit, ut legitur in libro. Et tamen, ut ex hoc die adhuc habetur in libro. Suspicor hoc est, quia est secundum ordinem et iustus. Dare fidem qua credit, est debitum. Autem, si non posset esse a forsit. Hoc forte est quod et singula verbo usus describere dictionary... inveniri potest in eius pages. Hoc videtur ordinate et iustus. Non solum in ordine.

Decem

Picture de caelo, non potest accipi. Hoc est utique, nisi caelum posset cover lorem ipsum dolor lens.

Undecim

Aliquid pulchra potest esse dixit, et etiam vidi. Quae duo posset providere maior description?

Duodecim

Usu an ferrum ferrum a shirt legit ironia ad usum est (scilicet a mathematician esset peritus hic cum introducti sumus verbum) ut par est, fructus canistrum cum divisa tomatoes.

12.08

Cum campana orbis sonus auditur, non quod de campana, sonus, quod campana producit. Multo sicut

logica, campana repraesentat responsum. Sonus est potius quaestio ad respondendum de bell.

12.10

Si pecunia est et pro quo mutatum bona, si bona fieri vel remanere "bonum" est? Pariter, si omnes est

"bonum" quare, ut nos interdum loqui, sic horrende "bonum" est.

Notes de Consideratione

Haec nota sunt cogitationes et considerationes varias quaestiones et locos, quae sustinere usum
Philosophiae trans et parallela cum necessitas cogitare.

Quomodo unum incipiunt intelligere docere? Docere est non iustus nobilis conatus justificationis inter
fratrem nostrum hominum. Docere est, ut adimpleretur quod sine cogitatione in mundo, universalis
curiositas. Hoc curiositas, ut impleretur per socialis distinctiones, philosophica complexities,
imaginariam mysterium & insidiaretur, et fortasse etiam per absoluta natura mathematica antidotes.
Quamquam artus refertur, unum in pace concludere, quod satis mensura aliqua necessitas docere hoc
labore esse constructum super docere(er) s voluntate, ut intelligere.

Docere aliquid, oportet intelligere. Intelligere, quod veritas indiget ad esse available. Est numquam
satis cognoscere, quid non est. Oportet sacrificium nostrum superbia ad hauriendam, ut prope et
intellectualiter potest intelligere et cognoscere, quod aliquid est. Quamvis epistemologically, ut
possimus invenire nostra methodus cognoscendi, nisi post nos determinare aliquid est. Ergo, ego erit
incipere logica et veritatis.

LOGICA & VERITATEM

Nos omnes a philosophia. Hoc philosophia nostra constituit, et regit multo nostrae cogitandi. Ut inveniamur in statu venit ad quasdam conclusiones nos ciere nostra philosophica prospectus per et cum regulas logica et ratiocinatio. Steven B. Cowan & Iacobum S. Speigel posuit illud hoc modo:

Logica est primum instrumentum philosophi. In logica, philosophus et posuit fundamentales et principales pro regendi suam ratus, pro dictating, quando et quomodo ad hauriendam conclusiones ex alia crediderunt, et pro aestimandis opiniones aliorum. Logica, in aliis verbis,, constituit scientia ratio.

In doctrina sciendum est, quod illic est a mensura. Hoc mensuram habet, a formula et quod formula servat, quos intelligere, cum a via aestimare, nova materia. Inveni maxima pericula in hodierna views Christiana regeneratione motus. Dum eius conatus facti bacchatur popularis in forma officia in dominica, horis matutinis, sed etiam coepit figura educational processus. Quomodo parens, doctor, discipulus tueri se ab huiusmodi impetus daemonum materia?

Praeterea nos a facie exstructa dimissione philosophica et rationis normam quae auxiliatus figura nostri leges regere homines cum postmodern motus. Hoc postmodern motus conatus ad infamiam ipsa fundamentum absolutum perspectivae, quae regunt cogitationes, affectus et passiones. Dr. John Warwici Montgomery insinuat:

Postmodernism, constet, an amorphous phaenomenon—magis quasi Novum, Age mentem: valde difficile est, ut suspenderet descendit propter hoc quod eius sectatores et hominibus viatoribus non esse unum credo. Sed unus of plurrimi utilis analyses phaenomenon fuerit provisum per D. E. Polkinghorne, qui agnoscit quattuor basic argumenta: (1) foundationlessness, (2) fragmentariness, (3) constructivism, et (4) neo-pragmatism. In Postmodernist, in servandum, ut nulla concretum epistemic fundamentum est, sese immediate et loci, et non in aliquo genere vera (quia sunt nemo); pro eo vel ea, nisi re productum est unum in alio construit, et quaestio non est utrum x verum est sed utrum accipiendo x unus erit devenire ad satis exitus.

Munus, ut puto, est unum, quod esset inventa prospera sub simplicitate. Tamen cogitans, nihil est, sed simplex. Is est an automated actione in ex ad collecta operatio coniungitur cum interiorem ostentationem exterius actio. Logica est fabula, et scientia est legenda. Forte, magister esset bene servivit ad dimittendum fabulosus status imaginari quid sit in fabulares mundi, quae fabulae vocant domum.

THE

BEGINNING

www.ingramcontent.com/pod-product-compliance
Lightning Source LLC
Chambersburg PA
CBHW070351290526
45791CB00003B/1501